STAY POSITIVE
WITH MARCUS AURELIUS

Jana Capri lives in Barcelona, Spain, speaks five languages and holds a degree in Translation and Interpretation from Charles University in Prague. She is a Master Practitioner in NLP (Neuro-Linguistic Programming) and has studied psychological astrology and creative writing. Jana is also a blogger and co-author of several books.

She has a strong interest in psychosomatics and personal growth and enjoys reading and writing books that inspire self-improvement and help others feel better about themselves.

Charan Díaz Arquillo is a psychologist based in Barcelona, Spain, with over twenty years of experience in psychotherapy, personal growth, educational psychology and organisational psychology. He holds a master's degree in Humanistic and Integrative Psychotherapy, as well as certifications in Mindfulness and Clinical Hypnosis from the University of Barcelona. Charan is also an author and co-author of several books.

He is passionate about Hindu and Greek philosophy, as well as oriental tales and mythology.

JANA CAPRI AND CHARAN DÍAZ

STAY POSITIVE WITH MARCUS AURELIUS

79 QUESTIONS AND ANSWERS FROM STOIC PHILOSOPHY

Published by Westland Books, a division of Nasadiya Technologies Private Limited, in 2025

No. 269/2B, First Floor, 'Irai Arul', Vimalraj Street, Nethaji Nagar, Alapakkam Main Road, Maduravoyal, Chennai 600095

Westland and the Westland logo are the trademarks of Nasadiya Technologies Private Limited, or its affiliates.

This English edition for the Indian Subcontinent published by arrangement with Suasive Consultants Private Limited (www.montsecortazar.com).

ISBN: 9789360456634

10 9 8 7 6 5

Typeset by Jojy Philip

Printed at Thomson Press (India) Ltd

CONTENTS

INTRODUCTION

During therapy, a patient posed the following question: how can you stay positive over the long term?

My intuitive response, after years dedicated to psychology, was: the only way to maintain a positive attitude is by continually exposing ourselves to a chosen positive inspiration, capable of influencing our way of thinking, speaking and acting. If you put wood on the fire, it will keep burning.

The idea that the mind is easily influenced and that it is possible to maintain a positive attitude in the long term led us to study the writings of Marcus Aurelius, a great Stoic philosopher and a role model for all who want to live more positive lives.

What better inspiration exists than that of the wise men of our history, who not only left us important advice in their writings, but also practised what they preached?

In *Stay Positive with Marcus Aurelius* we **combine modern psychology with philosophy** and spiritual ideas from across history.

When things go wrong for us, regardless of whether it is due to love, work, family, other relationships or health, Marcus Aurelius' messages can help us approach life from another perspective and raise our consciousness. Only with a heightened consciousness can an individual self-realise, self-transcend and, as a result, rise above the suffering that imprisons them.

HOW TO USE THIS BOOK

On the next page we explain the three parts of each chapter: (1) the question or comment of a seeker, (2) Marcus Aurelius' answer/message and (3) a psychological reflection.

By 'seeker' we mean all those who ask themselves about the mysteries of life and want to get answers based on this everlasting wisdom.

Marcus Aurelius' answers are inspired by his work *Meditations* and adapted to modern language for easy understanding.

The subsequent psychological reflection is food for thought, aiming to guide further deliberation on the messages of Marcus Aurelius. These suggested viewpoints should not be considered instructions or definitive interpretations of the Stoic messages, but rather invitations for the reader to pose questions and to consider elements that might help them to integrate the Stoic approach into their life.

1

PATHS WITH A HEART

Question/comment from a seeker:

Does the end justify the means? Sometimes I have to do things that I don't like, but that are necessary.

Response from Marcus Aurelius (VIII–V):

Remember that, most importantly, your duty is to always be a good person. When you have challenges to face or problems to solve, don't let them get to you or break you. Always look for the most humane solution: the one that allows you to be a good, modest, sincere and fair person.

Psychological Reflection

It is good to have a goal, but it must be a goal that is consistent with humaneness, that is, the ability to feel compassion or solidarity towards others, respecting human values.

Have you set significant goals in your life? Niccolò Machiavelli was not right: the end does not justify the means. The humane, kind and compassionate way to achieve a goal is more important than the goal itself. We need to have a clear conscience at the end of the day.

Analyse and examine your life: is there something you are currently trying to achieve, but that makes other people suffer or robs you of your peace of mind?

As the anthropologist Carlos Castaneda said, all paths are the same—they lead nowhere. But there are paths with a heart and paths without a heart.

Question or comment about life.

Marcus Aurelius' answer, based on his book *Meditations*. Reference to the original citation is in parentheses. Example: IV–XXIV: relevant excerpt can be found in Chapter 4, paragraph 24 of *Meditations*.

Psychological reflection to explore the message in more depth.

HOW TO GET THE MOST OUT OF THIS BOOK

We recommend that you use this book whenever:

- You are going through a difficult period in your life
- You're seeking positive inspiration
- You need more peace of mind, or to control anxiety, anger, sadness, etc.

You can select from the contents the chapter name that inspires you the most, or open the book at random and see which message you land upon.

The great philosophers of human history such as Seneca, Socrates, Marcus Aurelius, Epictetus and the Buddha help us understand that cultivating a desired mindset is not a matter of days, months or years, but rather life's work.

Despite this, it is worth the effort.

1

PATHS WITH A HEART

Question/comment from a seeker:

Does the end justify the means? Sometimes I have to do things that I don't like, but that are necessary.

Response from Marcus Aurelius (VIII–V):

Remember that, most importantly, your duty is to always be a good person. When you have challenges to face or problems to solve, don't let them get to you or break you. Always look for the most humane solution: the one that allows you to be a good, modest, sincere and fair person.

Psychological Reflection

It is good to have a goal, but it must be a goal that is consistent with humaneness, that is, the ability to feel compassion or solidarity towards others, respecting human values.

Have you set significant goals in your life? Niccolò Machiavelli was not right: the end does not justify the means. The humane, kind and compassionate way to achieve a goal is more important than the goal itself. We need to have a clear conscience at the end of the day.

Analyse and examine your life: is there something you are currently trying to achieve, but that makes other people suffer or robs you of your peace of mind?

As the anthropologist Carlos Castaneda said, all paths are the same—they lead nowhere. But there are paths with a heart and paths without a heart.

2

THE FIRST STEP IS TO WANT IT

Question/comment from a seeker:

What can I do to be happy and not feel frustrated? I feel very lost.

Response from Marcus Aurelius (VII–LXVII):

It takes very little to be happy. Perhaps you are taking a look at your life and thinking, 'I am very old and I am not famous or have much money, and I have not achieved anything important in life.' Keep learning and working on your human values, the quality of your relationships and your spirituality or inner freedom. That is the key to being happy and, besides, it is free.

Psychological Reflection

Would you like to improve any elements of your life? Do you want to improve anything related to your job, family, partner, health or money?

To change something, you first need to want to change. For example, imagine that someone tells a friend, 'I can't quit smoking.' At that very moment, a psychologist hears him and offers him free therapy to help stop smoking. And the smoker is quick to reply, 'But ... I don't want to quit smoking!'

To get anything in life, you have to want it first. If you really want to improve your life, sooner or later you will find a way to achieve it. As Marcus Aurelius says, it takes very little to be happy. You don't have to have a PhD, you just have to want to change.

3

WILLINGNESS TO LEARN

Question/comment from a seeker:

I'm already a certain age and have a lot of life experience, I don't need anyone to give me lessons.

Response from Marcus Aurelius (XI–XXIX):

Everything you know today, you have learnt by previously being a student. You need to understand that in life, to become a master, you will first have to be a humble apprentice.

Psychological Reflection

A learning mindset is a springboard for your growth. When you believe you know everything, in reality you are more limited and listen less carefully to everything around you. When your intention is to learn, you observe and pay attention to your surroundings and, as a result, perceive reality more clearly and are more successful in your actions.

Do you remember a time when, thanks to your desire to learn, you improved a skill?

A learning and growth mindset helps you be happier and have more freedom to react to whatever comes your way.

The University of Life wants you to always seek to learn. The choice is yours.

4

DOING THE RIGHT THING

Question/comment from a seeker:

What can I do to resist the influence of others when they lead me astray?

Response from Marcus Aurelius (XII–XVII):

If something is not in accordance with your values, don't do it. You must analyse the situation yourself and decide what is right.

Psychological Reflection

Deep down, you already know what is right and what is wrong. An adult human being knows, at the very least, that he should not do to others what he does not want done to himself. That said, sometimes we like to 'play dumb' or pretend that we don't know many things.

Does what you think, do and say at this moment in your life feel ethical enough or can it be improved?

What prevents you right here and now from improving some aspects of your life, in order to do what you consider more correct, more humane? Is there anything in your life that you don't really think is correct, but you do anyway because 'everyone is doing it'? What can you change to move closer to a more authentic life?

It is very difficult to be happy without human values.

5

GOODNESS

Question/comment from a seeker:

The world is unfair. Why aren't good people rewarded more? I do many things for others but I am not always valued.

Response from Marcus Aurelius (IX–XLII):

Don't expect anything in return or seek a reward when you do something nice for others. It would be just as strange as your feet asking you for a reward for walking, or your eyes for seeing.

The nature of the human being is to do good, and that is why you were born. When you are a good person, you are in tune with your essence. Don't expect to receive a reward for it, try to be a good person sincerely and naturally.

Psychological Reflection

Goodness is part of your nature. According to research on positive psychology, when you are good you are happier, and when you are happier you generally want to do more good.

Have you ever done something nice for someone else without expecting anything in return? How did you feel afterwards?

6

CHASING THE EPHEMERAL

Question/comment from a seeker:

It may sound selfish, but the things and people around me are the most important to me—my possessions, my house, my car, the people I love … nothing else matters much to me.

Response from Marcus Aurelius (IV–III):

Observe how quickly life passes. Before you existed, eternity already existed, and it will continue to exist when you leave this world. From this perspective, everything else loses importance (other people, your possessions, your problems …). We are temporary beings with temporary problems.

Psychological Reflection

We live in a fast-paced, 'liquid' world where everything is constantly changing. A world in which we are 'infoxicated'—intoxicated by the excess of ever-changing information. An uncertain, unstable and chaotic world.

How do you find stability and serenity in this world? Do you seek it by pleasing others, do you seek it in money, in power, in travel, in varied enjoyable experiences?

Why run after the empty, ephemeral and meaningless things, if life can change in an instant, meaning that you will rapidly lose everything or have to leave all of it behind?

Seek serenity within yourself. You can look for it, for example, in meditation, or develop psychological resources and build mental strength. In this way, nothing external will disturb your peace.

7

TAKE IT PHILOSOPHICALLY

Question/comment from a seeker:

I have a major problem that makes me very anxious. What can I do to better deal with it and not feel so much stress?

Response from Marcus Aurelius (IV–III):

These two points will help you feel freer and more relaxed:

1) What really makes you suffer is your opinion—what you think about yourself, your thoughts about others, about life and about your problems. Life is objective and external, but your internal opinion is subjective and can make you suffer if you don't manage it well.
2) Everything you see and everything that happens to you is constantly changing and disappearing (transforming). I'm sure you have seen this happening throughout your life. The quality of your life depends on how you

manage your opinion about everything that changes and transforms around you (the way you see and judge what happens to you).

Psychological Reflection

The possibility of you suffering due to any reason depends on the way you approach the situation, your opinion about it and your ability to accept the state of affairs. Learning to take what happens to you in a philosophical way and with optimism will always keep you better in touch with your life, and it will be easier for you to achieve good things.

Think of something that bothers you or causes you stress or anxiety at this time in your life. Is it really the fact or the situation itself that disturbs you? Or is it just the opinion that you have about that situation that makes you feel negative?

8

USELESS THINGS

Question/comment from a seeker:

How can I maintain a good mood?

Response from Marcus Aurelius (IV–XXIV):

If you want to be in a good mood, don't do too many things.

Most of the things you think, do and say are not as necessary as you think. If you reduce them, you will have more free time and will be calmer.

Ask yourself the following questions regularly: is this really necessary? Is it useful?

Unnecessary thoughts lead to useless actions, and you fall into a loop which then disrupts your well-being.

Psychological Reflection

Among all you have said, done or thought today, has anything been useless or unnecessary?

For example, how can you disconnect so that you don't dwell on repetitive thoughts so much that you end up getting nowhere? How could you speak and act in a more practical way the next time a situation occurs where you tend to react badly?

9

INNER STRENGTH

Question/comment from a seeker:

I have tasks to manage and responsibilities to assume, but feel neither the courage nor the strength to do what I have to do.

Response from Marcus Aurelius (VI–XXIX):

It is a shame that at this moment in your life, when your body has not yet failed you, your soul has already surrendered.

Psychological Reflection

What good is willpower if you don't use it? Willpower is a muscle that strengthens when used regularly. It is up to you to find your inner strength, which inspires you and elevates your life. And learning to feed your fire on a daily basis is your responsibility.

What could give you the strength to master your tasks and responsibilities well?

What are you: a body or a soul? Your inner strength is much greater than you think.

10

CLEAR CONSCIENCE

Question/comment from a seeker:

How can you keep calm in a world filled with so many ill-intentioned people?

Response from Marcus Aurelius (VI–XLVII):

Focus on what is most important: be honest with yourself and with others. Be a good person. Develop tolerance for people who lie or are unjust, as you can't avoid them. Don't let their toxic behaviour influence you.

Psychological Reflection

Imagine that you travel to a world where only liars and unjust people exist. Living among them, do you think you should forget your values and conscience? In our day-to-day lives, we meet all kinds of people. Some people have a good impact on us, some do not. It is important that you do not compromise on your principles as a result of negative influences, because a clear conscience is priceless.

11

THE SECRET TO A GOOD LIFE

Question/comment from a seeker:

Can you give me some advice so that events in my life don't affect me so much?

Response from Marcus Aurelius (XI–XVI):

The potential to live your best life lies in the soul, and the strength of your inner self depends on you.

Whatever happens in your life, everything is external, unchangeable; it has not been imposed on your inner self and there is no value in judging it.

Leave your inner page blank and if any judgement appears, erase it instantly.

Psychological Reflection

Tell me what you love and I'll tell you who you are. Where is your attention focused most of the day? There are people preoccupied with their clothes, their house, their prestige, wealth, sex, food, their favourite TV series ... this is what their mind contains.

Your mind is with you twenty-four hours a day, seven days a week. Appreciate the value of your life by remembering that you are not eternal and that nothing will be.

Here is a question that can help you in many situations in life: what is the most important thing to consider, what should I focus on?

12

THE NATURE OF THINGS

Question/comment from a seeker:

Often, I end up suffering because I don't understand the reason why something happens. For example, why does someone get angry with me, or why is it up to me to take on the burden of doing certain tasks ...

Response from Marcus Aurelius (XII–X):

It is not always possible to understand everything. Take an objective point of view. Observe things as they really are, analyse their cause, their relationship and their essence. Taking an unbiased standpoint will make you feel better.

Psychological Reflection

Everything is interrelated. Understanding this can help us discover the multi-dimensional nature of our well-being. The interpretations you make about what is happening in your life, your thoughts, your emotions, your attitude and your behaviour are all interrelated, and they do not exist separately. To understand a certain type of behaviour, we must analyse the thoughts that accompany it.

Think about the last time you acted poorly—can you remember the thoughts and emotions that led you to act in this way? And what thoughts and emotions were the strongest the last time you remember being kind and patient?

13

THE SPARK WITHIN

Question/comment from a seeker:

I'm not interested in spirituality. I don't understand why it is useful.

Response from Marcus Aurelius (III–XIII):

Doctors always have at hand the instruments and devices necessary for an emergency intervention. We must always have at hand the ability to take care of your divine (spiritual) and human (earthly) sides.

Always remember that even when it comes to seemingly insignificant matters, there is a relationship between spirituality and the world around us.

Everything you achieve on an earthly level should correspond with the care of your spiritual side.

Psychological Reflection

Faced with many materialistic and worldly problems, we tend to forget what is most sacred to us, what we value or love most in our lives.

If you put wood on a fire, it will keep burning. Systematically surround yourself with people who inspire you, read books or texts that encourage you and guide yourself to visualise what elevates you internally. Will your inner spark or strength go out while you continue to add fuel to it?

14

THE ORIGIN OF EVERYTHING

Question/comment from a seeker:

Does it make sense to believe in God or in some other higher being or entity?

Response from Marcus Aurelius (VI–XXXVI):

Reflect on the origin of everything. Your purpose as a human being and your self-realisation may lie in learning to see the spiritual origin of everything around you.

Psychological Reflection

Often, we are so focused on our lives that we forget to reflect on the engine that drives everything.

Most of the great sages and philosophers in the history of humanity consider existence to be useless if time is not dedicated to meditation or to serious reflection on what moves the universe, what you were before you were born and what you will be after death. If a child forgets to relate to their father and does not know how to reconnect with him, they will not know what to do when they need that connection the most.

What spiritual practice can you incorporate into your routine to live a fuller life?

15

KNOW YOURSELF

Question/comment from a seeker:

How can I worry less?

Response from Marcus Aurelius (VII–XVII):

Your happiness consists of tuning in to your *daimon* (inner wisdom). Don't let your stability be disrupted by your imagination. If you worry about problems that do not exist yet, you will be better off thinking, 'Get out of here, imagination! Don't distract me by inventing worries. I won't get angry with you, but go away.'

Psychological Reflection

Happiness depends on you discovering your true identity. We are not our job, our possessions or what we usually identify with. We have a soul, but we are not always sufficiently in tune with it to be permanently happy.

Imagination is a double-edged sword, and it confuses us when it is misused. Excessive worry or anxiety are errors of imagination. So are depression and other types of emotional stress, which can lead us to give too much urgency or importance to things, or to exaggerate and demand too much of ourselves, others or life.

Only by understanding who we really are beyond the standard labels, and having faith in the meaning of life, will we begin to comprehend the happiness that philosophers talk about.

Know yourself, be optimistic, do your best, do not stress and forget about the rest.

16

YOUR INNER GARDEN

Question/comment from a seeker:

How can I have a more positive attitude towards life?

Response from Marcus Aurelius (VIII–XLIII):

I like to cultivate my inner wisdom. Learn to appreciate and look with kindness at reality and at people. This way, you will have the right perspective and be able to attribute to everything the value it really has.

Psychological Reflection

Is anything more enjoyable than a good inner environment or climate? Imagine that tomorrow is a beautiful day—a fantastic summer sun is shining, people are smiling and you are surrounded by beauty ... but inside, you are in a bad mood and everything appears to you as though it is garbage.

If you learn to care for and keep your 'inner garden' in optimal condition and your 'internal climate' is right for you, even if tomorrow is a cloudy and rainy day and other people are angry, everything will go well. Then, it will be easier for you to be happy and calm, engaging better with others.

Every day, observe and differentiate the mentality that hurts you from the one that benefits you to enjoy your inner garden despite external difficulties.

17

THE IMPORTANT PART IS INSIDE YOU

Question/comment from a seeker:

Sometimes, I find myself placing too much importance on my body. I spend too much time exercising, taking care of my appearance, dressing well ...

Is that a bad thing?

Response from Marcus Aurelius (X–XXXVIII):

Never confuse your spirit with the container it is in, with the limbs or organs that give it a physical form. Your body is an instrument and, without your soul, it has no more use than the cloth without the weaver, the pen without the writer or the steering wheel without the driver.

Remember that the important part is inside you.

Psychological Reflection

If you identify with your body, with your opinions, your emotions or with what you possess, you have a problem because all that can change.

It is better that you put your energy and your determination into the things that do not change or in the things that depend only on you. For example, your fighting spirit depends only on you. Your will to be a better person depends only on you. What you do to cheer yourself up when you're sad is up to you. What moves you is not your body, but the spirit that you feed.

Think of something that depends only on you, and what you could do to improve your life or to achieve a goal that you have set for yourself. At the same time, think about what does not depend on you at all.

18

YOUR TRUE VALUE

Question/comment from a seeker:

How can I avoid having so many emotional ups and downs in my life?

Response from Marcus Aurelius (XII–XIX):

It is time to realise that you have within you something more powerful and divine than what moves your passions and makes you dance to their music.

Psychological Reflection

You can start by appreciating all the good that already exists within you and accepting that you can achieve wonderful things in your life.

You are more than your emotions and passions, because you have the ability to think, discern, analyse and evaluate. Do not let your emotions dominate you or shake you like a doll, as Marcus Aurelius advises us.

Is there an area in your life where you should use your reasoning and logic more and not get carried away so much by your emotions?

19

THE WISE

Question/comment from a seeker:

How can I be the best version of myself?

Response from Marcus Aurelius (IV–XXXVIII):

Look closely at the principles that guide the sages to understand what they avoid and what they pursue in life.

Psychological Reflection

Who is a wise person in your eyes and what does this wise person want from life?

The history of humanity has thousands of examples of 'wise men' such as Socrates, Buddha, Confucius, Lao Tzu, Plato, Seneca, Epictetus and Marcus Aurelius. What did they seek? Weren't they looking for the best from life?

Can't you learn from their values and optimism, to take things with more serenity and less drama? If you try to imitate them, won't you be a better human being?

If it is not natural for you to seek more wisdom yourself, perhaps you can try to learn from the wise, in order to suffer less and be happier.

20

AN EYE FOR AN EYE

Question/comment from a seeker:

They say revenge is sweet.

Response from Marcus Aurelius (VI–VI):

The best way to defend yourself from people who offend you is to not be like them.

Psychological Reflection

If you take an approach of 'tit for tat', will you be any different from the person who harmed you in the first place? As stated by Gandhi, an eye for an eye makes the whole world blind. According to *The Book of Mirdad*, we live in order to learn to love and we love in order to learn to live.

So, the best defence will be to learn to love and forgive. But that does not mean we should allow ourselves to be mistreated or put up with abusive behaviour. We can have compassion but we must take care of our well-being.

21

IT IS NOT PERSONAL

Question/comment from a seeker:

What can I think or do so that I don't take everything so seriously?

Response from Marcus Aurelius (IX–IV):

He who commits a fault, commits it against himself. He who commits an injustice, harms himself.

Psychological Reflection

Often, when we are criticised or insulted, we take it personally. When someone hurts us or when we believe we are not being treated fairly, we usually take it to heart. We feel the injustice and misfortune, and we perceive ourselves as the victims of the situation.

However, Marcus Aurelius tells us that he who acts badly hurts himself. He who tries to harm another only harms himself. Every thought, word and action returns like a boomerang to the person who has thought, spoken or acted badly.

Have you ever felt wronged because of some injustice that you thought was dealt to you, and then realised later that in actual fact, it didn't have anything to do with you?

22

KINDNESS AND COMPASSION

Question/comment from a seeker:

There are people in the world who are very ignorant. How can I relate to them?

Response from Marcus Aurelius (II–XIII):

Sometimes you should also feel compassion for those people who have lost their way in life, as they are like a blind person who cannot distinguish black from white. Their ignorance prevents them from differentiating between good and bad.

Psychological Reflection

We live in a time when people feel disorderly love, as Saint John of the Cross said. This means that the hierarchy of values that most people have leads them to more suffering instead of peace of mind, wisdom and well-being. People waste their lives pursuing goals such as money, power or pleasurable experiences, only to discover later that they have wasted their lives chasing after things that did not give them lasting inner fulfilment or happiness.

Marcus Aurelius explains that this is why kindness and compassion towards everyone is so important. We are all souls in search of peace, we all experience situations of suffering, and we cannot imagine what other people are going through. As Jesus said, 'Father, forgive them; for they know not what they do.'

23

TO WHOM DO YOU LISTEN?

Question/comment from a seeker:

I worry too much about what other people think. How can I improve my confidence and self-esteem?

Response from Marcus Aurelius (XII–IV):

How can you say that you respect yourself if you give more importance to others' opinion than to your own?

Psychological Reflection

Why pay more attention to what others think about you if it limits and discourages you from achieving positive things in your life and from loving yourself?

Remember a situation in your life when you felt rejected (by your partner, parents, a friend, at work, etc.). What have you learnt from that experience?

24

AUTHENTIC LISTENING

Question/comment from a seeker:

I have to relate to people who are very different to me. There is no chemistry, we do not understand each other … What can I do to better connect with them?

Response from Marcus Aurelius (VI–LIII):

Practise listening very carefully to what others are saying and try to see things from the speaker's perspective.

Psychological Reflection

Imagine someone who, at the end of summer, asks his or her co-worker how their holidays went. But before hearing the answer, they begin to recount their own vacation. That co-worker will discover with disappointment that the question was just a way for the person to discuss their own holiday under the false disguise of wanting to listen. What that person really wanted was for someone to attend to them.

Authentic listening requires attention, concentration, genuine interest and empathy. When you listen to someone, are you aware of the objective of the other person's communication? Maybe that person just wants to express their emotions, get recognition, feel acknowledged or have someone by their side.

We all appreciate people who are genuine and good listeners. Do you remember a conversation you had with someone who really made you feel like they were listening to you? What made you feel this way?

25

AFTER DEATH

Question/comment from a seeker:

Isn't the idea of death terrifying to you?

Response from Marcus Aurelius (II–XI):

Leaving this world is not a terrible prospect. If the spirit world exists, nothing bad will happen to you. But if the Divine does not exist or we humans are insignificant, does it really matter that we are leaving an empty world that has no spiritual sense?

Psychological Reflection

Marcus Aurelius offers us a thought to help us feel calmer about a subject that has almost become a taboo in our current society: death.

He invites us to reflect on the idea that there are only two options. One is that there is something else out there when we die (something that philosophers have devoted their entire lives to, investigating practices that they called initiation into the mysteries of life and death). The second alternative is that nothing exists.

If nothing exists, why bother? According to Marcus Aurelius, a world in which nothing exists after death is, in a way, a world without meaning. And if there *is* something, you should act in this life as the gods, or God, would want if they were constantly watching you. Act in such a way that if one day you have to meet God face-to-face, it will be a pleasant encounter.

26

THE PERFECT ORDER

Question/comment from a seeker:

Sometimes, I think that life is meaningless.

Response from Marcus Aurelius (II–III):

You are part of something greater than yourself, something that we call nature or life. During our time on earth, things happen that we may not understand but which preserve the perfect order of this superior system.

Everything that happens contributes to a greater good and has a meaning.

Psychological Reflection

Everything in this world is related, intertwined. Nothing happens by chance and everything is in a perfect order that we humans are incapable of understanding. So, wouldn't it be better to have faith in that order and trust that everything that is inevitable is just as it should be?

Life has meaning regardless of whether we believe in it or not.

27

THE DURATION OF LIFE

Question/comment from a seeker:

I prefer to think that I still have a long time to live. Nobody wants to think about death.

Response from Marcus Aurelius (II–XI):

Remember that you will not live forever: act, speak and think as if you were about to leave this life. If you do so, your priorities will be clearer and you will manage your time better.

Psychological Reflection

What would you do if you knew for sure that you had little time left to live? How would you treat your loved ones? How would your priorities change?

Live each day as if it were your last, prioritising what really matters in life.

28

GIVE YOUR BEST PERFORMANCE

Question/comment from a seeker:

What can I do to better accept uncertainty when I am in the midst of my life crises?

Response from Marcus Aurelius (IV–XXVI):

What happens to you is not up to you. Accept everything that happens to you and that you cannot control, because all of it has been predetermined by 'universal nature'. It is better to focus on the positive elements that you can control, to help solve each crisis.

Psychological Reflection

You are simply the interpreter of a role assigned to you by the 'director'. You don't write the film and you don't know the complete script, nor do you have the ability to change any part of it. You are just one actor among a multitude of actors.

Do you think the film will change just because you don't like the scene that you were chosen to participate in? But even when you can't alter what happens, you can nonetheless choose the best approach and reaction to it. That will change everything.

You are not the director, but you are the protagonist of the film. Perform the best version of your role.

29

EMBRACE EVERYTHING

Question/comment from a seeker:

Isn't accepting my destiny the same as conforming, which is not a good thing? I don't think that the bad things that happen to me necessarily have a silver lining.

Response from Marcus Aurelius (V–VIII):

When you accept what fate offers you and try to manage the inevitable, you do so in the hope of evolving, since everything that happens to you has a meaning, even if you don't understand it.

Would it help you to avoid taking the medicine that a doctor offers you to improve your health? In the same way that a doctor can recommend certain unpleasant activities and medicines to improve your health, the unpleasant circumstances that life or the universe sends your way also have their purpose. You should take them with the understanding that they will help you improve as a human being.

Psychological Reflection

Saint Pio of Pietrelcina shared a story: A mother is embroidering. Her son, seated on a small stool, contemplates her work but from the back, and sees the knots in the embroidery and the scrambled threads. He says, 'Mum, what are you doing? Your work is messy!' Then the mother lowers the hoop and shows her son the good side of the embroidery. Each colour is in its place and the variety of threads reflects the harmony of the design. This is exactly what Marcus Aurelius' words are about! We see the backside of the embroidery; we are sitting on a low stool.

How would your life improve if you had more faith in everything that you don't understand? What would you be like if you had greater confidence in your abilities to accept, learn, grow and evolve?

30

THINGS YOU CANNOT CONTROL

Question/comment from a seeker:

I panic about everything that I cannot control: my partner leaving me, being fired from work, becoming sick ...

Response from Marcus Aurelius (V–XXXV):

Ask yourself this question: if you've done your best and acted with the most sincere intentions, but something unfortunate still happens to you, why should you care?

Psychological Reflection

If something happens that is not within your control, accept it. We rely much more on chance than we think. So what is the point of blaming ourselves for what we cannot control? Wouldn't it be better if we put all our energy and efforts into things that we can manage?

Is there something in your life that worries you but that you cannot control?

31

THINGS ARE AS THEY ARE

Question/comment from a seeker:

There are things about my body and my personality that I find difficult to accept.

Response from Marcus Aurelius (VI–XXXIX):

Get used to what destiny has chosen for you.

Psychological Reflection

As Jesus said, even the hairs on our heads have been numbered. There is also a Hindu proverb that says that each grain of rice is inscribed with the name of the person who will eat it. Meanwhile, a Zen attitude offers us the following approach: if you understand, things are as they are. If you don't understand, things are as they are.

However, we allow ourselves to be carried away by the illusion of control, believing that we can change many things.

What attitude could help you accept everything that comes your way in life?

32

EXTERNAL CRITICISM

Question/comment from a seeker:

I am very easily offended by people's criticism. What can I do?

Response from Marcus Aurelius (IV–XI):

When someone offends you, do not allow yourself to interpret things the way that person does or let them change your own opinion. Just look at things objectively, as they really are.

Psychological Reflection

We should not be swayed by the opinions of others that are intended to offend. If you remain calm in the face of such situations and are patient, there will only be one fool. But if you allow yourself to be carried away by your anger and react with aggression, there will be two fools.

If a deranged person praises you, saying you are God, or insults you, saying you are Satan, are you likely to listen to them? You can take the same approach in real life when someone tries to offend you.

If you lend too much weight to the criticisms of others, it will end up becoming a burden to you.

33

PEACE OF MIND

Question/comment from a seeker:

I am a very ambitious person. I would like to have a successful career, full of recognition at work so that I can gratify my desires and indulge in all the pleasures that I want, and not have to deprive myself of anything. Is that bad?

Response from Marcus Aurelius (VI–LI):

He who delights in fame depends on what others do or say about him. He who adores pleasure depends on his passions. He who worships wisdom depends on his own actions.

Be careful what you pursue. Only when you seek introspection and wisdom will you achieve self-realisation and be truly free.

Psychological Reflection

It is important to understand what happiness means to you and how you can aim to be happy.

Sometimes we believe that if we are successful professionally, we will be happy. Or if we were rich or if we had a child ... then we would be happy. But ... are there not people who are professionally successful, rich, have children and still feel frustrated, empty and unhappy? This happens because they look for happiness in the wrong place: they look for it on the outside instead of on the inside. As the Dalai Lama has taught us, peace of mind and wisdom have to be created by yourself.

Who would you prefer to be: an ambitious person or someone with peace of mind? The choice is yours.

34

PLEASING OTHERS

Question/comment from a seeker:

I have sacrificed a lot for others and now I realise that it has become difficult for me to prioritise myself.

Response from Marcus Aurelius (VII–XXXIV):

Notice how curious the mind is. Observe the nature of other people's thoughts, notice what people are like, what they avoid and what they pursue, and how they spend their energy on all this.

However, everything changes quickly, like the sand on the seashore, which is swiftly covered by more sand carried by the wind and waves.

Do not let your past affect you, because everything is temporary.

Psychological Reflection

Let's take the example of a person who places too much importance on pleasing others. He is concerned that people will think badly of him and tries very hard to be liked, sacrificing himself and no longer being true to his values. In his last days, he realises that he has not lived his own life; he has lived a life for others and this sacrifice was not worth it.

Marcus Aurelius reminds us how fleeting or ephemeral everything in life is. While the opinion of others lasts a very short time, like something written on sand, taking care of your values and your conscience is something long-lasting, like etchings on a rock.

35

YOU ARE IN CONTROL

Question/comment from a seeker:

Sometimes, I allow myself to be manipulated by others because I don't have the courage to say no.

Response from Marcus Aurelius (V–X):

These two thoughts can reassure you:

Nothing will happen to you that is not already predetermined. Everything will happen according to the order of the universe.

No one can force you to do something against your values or your inner god. You are always in control of your actions.

Psychological Reflection

Can someone get you to be unfaithful to yourself, to your principles and your virtues, and persuade you to stop listening to your soul, without your consent?

It is only you who can think, speak or act against your own will.

36

INTROSPECTION

Question/comment from a seeker:

What can I do when everyday problems (work, family, emotions, etc.) prevent me from ever recharging my energy? I am always exhausted and stressed out.

Response from Marcus Aurelius (VI–XII):

You can take it philosophically. If you had a stepmother and your real mother, you might respect the former but would probably be more comfortable with the latter. It is the same with worldly activities and philosophy. Always comfort yourself in the arms of true philosophy and always return to it. Philosophy will make it easier for you to cope with the world's happenings and its problems.

Psychological Reflection

Even Superman went to a resting place so that he could recharge his strength. In these modern times, we can practise meditation and other introspective exercises that help the brain and body recover to optimal levels through deliberate rest. There are also philosophies or ways of perceiving the world that can help you de-dramatise situations and live more healthily. It is very likely that Marcus Aurelius engaged in both practices.

How about you? How do you recharge your batteries?

37

EVERYTHING HAS ITS BEAUTY

Question/comment from a seeker:

This world is becoming worse with time.

Response from Marcus Aurelius (III–II):

It can be helpful to remember that even the things you dislike about nature or life, and everything that happens to you, contains a certain beauty. Everything that comes about in life has its own charm for those who are able to appreciate it.

Psychological Reflection

An artificial flower can be aesthetically very beautiful, but when you try to smell it, you discover that it does not have the perfume of a real flower. In the same way, you can ask yourself: who am I? Would I know how to find the parts of myself that have grace and charm? Would I know how to find it in others and in life?

If the Creator is perfect, mustn't his creation and everything that happens in it be perfect as well?

38

FORGIVENESS

Question/comment from a seeker:

I find forgiveness hard.

Response from Marcus Aurelius (IV–III):

All rational beings have to put up with each other if they want to be kind and fair and live in harmony.

Bear in mind that many people have fallen out with others, have caused suspicion, hatred and conflict. But today, many of these people are already in their graves and are nothing more than dust.

Life is short; stop getting angry.

Psychological Reflection

Given that life is short and passes very quickly, how long do you want to hold on to a grudge towards someone? Who suffers more due to the resentment—you or the other person?

When you are angry, forgiveness is the only remedy. When you sincerely forgive, the first person who benefits is you, by shedding the burden of that grievance. We can forgive other people, ourselves, life, a company, etc.—anything we are angry at. Forgiveness has no limits.

If forgiveness is so good for your emotions and your mind, why don't you try to practise it more often? Is there someone or something in your life that you need to forgive? How would you feel if you did?

39

OPINIONS OF OTHERS

Question/comment from a seeker:

I have to admit that I like gossiping. I want to know what is going on in others' lives and sometimes I catch myself criticising others ...

Response from Marcus Aurelius (IV–XVIII):

A person gains a lot of free time when they do not look at what others say, do or think, and instead focus on their own actions.

Take what you don't like about others and try to improve those aspects in your own character.

Psychological Reflection

How much time and energy would we save if we paid less attention to others? Stop reflecting on what others think and worry about being a good person with values and virtues.

If you are interested in your own personal growth, take the aspects that you do not like in other people and work on these in your personality. Ask yourself: what can I improve this week in myself that I don't like in others?

40

DO NOT GO OFF TRACK

Question/comment from a seeker:

When I feel that others doubt me, my abilities and my strengths, I often lose motivation and find myself unable to achieve the goals that I set for myself.

Response from Marcus Aurelius (IV–XVIII):

Do not get distracted by the things around you. Run in a straight line without wandering. This will make it easier for you to reach your goals.

Psychological Reflection

Instead of judging others, observe yourself. Get in the habit of focusing on your own strengths, rather than the weaknesses of others. If one wins a war, it will be because of their power, not their weaknesses.

Those who say that something cannot be achieved should not interrupt those who are already doing it. If you know that you are achieving something positive, why let those who do not believe in you discourage you?

Whenever you pursue a goal, you will find barriers that will try to stop or distract you, or people who will criticise you along the way. You might come across obstacles that divert you from your aims.

If you get distracted, be aware of this and accept it: 'I've been distracted.' Next, seek to re-balance yourself: redirect your attention, your thoughts, your emotions and your actions back to the path that will open positive doors in your life.

41

HAVE YOUR OWN PERSPECTIVE

Question/comment from a seeker:

Sometimes, when I am with my family, I wonder whether it is better to adapt and establish harmony, or to say and do what I consider correct and stand up to them ...

Response from Marcus Aurelius (IV–XLVI):

You can respect your family and, at the same time, be aware that you should not blindly accept their damaging and negative opinions just because 'they are family'. Nor is it good to justify your bad actions by stating that 'this is how I have been educated'.

You are responsible for your actions and you have the power to choose.

Psychological Reflection

Do you sometimes do something just because 'it's always been done this way', or repeat what others say or do without reflecting upon whether those words or actions mirror the truth?

Marcus Aurelius encourages us to have our own perspective. We must listen to others and consider what they say, but never blindly follow their opinions and advice.

Think about something your parents or others close to you used to say a lot during your childhood. The mind of a child is like a sponge that absorbs everything that they see and hear. Quite often, we accept their viewpoints and adopt them without proper reflection. If we consider them now, we might find that we have differing opinions.

Sometimes we copy others without realising it, because we have become accustomed to doing so. Is there something that you have 'adopted' from the people around you, but you would actually be better off thinking or acting differently?

42

APPROVAL AND CRITICISM

Question/comment from a seeker:

When I do not achieve success in life or the approval of others, I feel worthless and like a failure.

Response from Marcus Aurelius (VIII–LII):

There are many people who are very lost in this world. There are people who do not know what the true purpose of being human is, do not understand how this world works or where they really are ... they do not even think about it.

Does it make sense to seek the approval of people who are shallow and lost?

Psychological Reflection

What is the point of seeking applause or fearing criticism from superficial people who are not interested in understanding the mysteries of this world, who do not know anything about existence and who do not have a virtuous purpose in their own life?

It is easy to do and say what others like and receive 'likes' as a result. But this will not make you happy in the long run. Not only because you cannot always please everyone, but also because true and lasting happiness comes from within yourself, not the people around you.

Are you searching for someone's approval? What if you did what feels right to you, regardless of what that person thinks? How would you feel?

43

SEEK THE TRUTH

Question/comment from a seeker:

What is better: that people tell you the truth even if it is painful or that they tell you a white lie to prevent you from suffering? What about constructive criticism?

Response from Marcus Aurelius (VI–XXI):

I am a seeker of the truth and I think that the truth has never hurt anyone. What hurts us is self-deception and ignorance.

That said, if someone criticises my behaviour because I have deviated from the truth and they try to help me rectify this, I will gladly accept that criticism.

Psychological Reflection

We all have the capacity to discern the truth and choose how we react, how we can be deliberate in our thought process and what decisions we need to make in different situations in life.

On many occasions, we face external criticism. We can choose how to react to it: we can get angry and let ourselves be carried away by pride, or we can contemplate whether there is some good sense in the criticism, which could help us grow. In the end, as the Buddha said, even if someone offers you many dishes, you will be the one choosing which ones you eat and which you leave. Criticism is somewhat similar.

Do you remember any criticism that has helped you correct or improve something? Have you put aside any criticism, like a dish that you have decided not to eat? Which option did you choose in different situations and why?

44

LIFE CHANGES

Question/comment from a seeker:

I am afraid of change. I am comfortable with my current situation and I want everything to stay as it is.

Response from Marcus Aurelius (VII–XVIII):

Why are you worried about change? Can anything really happen if there is no change?

Observe the changes in nature. It is impossible to light a fire without transforming firewood. For your body to digest something implies the transformation of the food we eat. Can a vital process take place without changing something?

For nature and life, changes are necessary and inevitable. The same applies to human beings.

Psychological Reflection

As Heraclitus says, change is the only constant. Everything in this world is constantly changing. Even as you are reading this, a lot of changes are happening in your body, because if there is no change, there is no life.

What are some changes that you once feared happening, but has come to pass since then and led to you enjoying a better life?

45

YOUR GRAIN OF SAND

Question/comment from a seeker:

I feel like I'm not making progress in life. No matter how hard I try, I don't notice any significant improvement. How can I prevent myself from becoming frustrated?

Response from Marcus Aurelius (IX–XXIX):

What you can do is limit yourself to what nature demands of you in each moment. Do not think that you are going to establish a great empire like Plato's Republic. Do what you have to do without being distracted by comparing yourself with others or looking at people around you.

Be satisfied with even the slightest progress and celebrate the result—it is no small thing.

Psychological Reflection

You are not going to change the world, you are not going to establish a system of perfect justice, nor are you going to convince others to see the world through your eyes.

If you feel you want to do something meaningful, maybe you can make yourself useful to someone, help somebody or bring cheer to those around you. If you can do your bit to assist another human being, why not do it?

What opportunities do you have right now to help improve the lives of others, which you are not currently using?

46

ADJUST YOUR EXPECTATIONS

Question/comment from a seeker:

If we were all good people, there would be no problems in the world. But these days, people are only interested in taking advantage of others. We live in a very selfish society ...

Response from Marcus Aurelius (IX–XLII):

If you meet someone who is dishonest or worthless, ask yourself: could it ever be possible not to have any evil people in this world? It's not. So don't demand the impossible. You can remind yourself of this phrase: this is one of the dishonest people who are an inevitable part of this world.

Psychological Reflection

If we accept that there are ignorant people in the world, why are we surprised when we meet such a person? Do we think we are in some way special and that strange people or those with bad intentions will never approach us?

It is always good to adjust your expectations to reality.

You always have the power to choose how you react to what reality presents to you.

47

WHAT MATTERS IS YOUR ATTITUDE

Question/comment from a seeker:

I am a loser, everything seems to be working against me. They fired me from work. What am I going to do with my life now?

Response from Marcus Aurelius (IV–XLIX):

When a misfortune happens to you and you complain about it, does the situation prevent you from being honest, authentic, kind, humble or from having hope, trust and all the virtues that are part of human nature?

Every time you are upset, remember: having to go through an uncomfortable situation is not a disgrace; rather, the ability to take it philosophically is a virtue.

Psychological Reflection

You can't control what happens to you, but you can shape your attitude towards it. Can external events prevent you from maintaining a positive outlook?

Think of someone who has had to endure some misfortune and, in spite of this, has managed to stay positive. What can you learn from that person?

48

GET BACK ON THE RIGHT TRACK

Question/comment from a seeker:

I have made a mistake and I feel very guilty about it.

Response from Marcus Aurelius (V–IX):

Do not be upset, or give up or be discouraged if you have strayed from the right path. When you fail, learn from your mistakes and get yourself back on track. You will feel satisfied if your actions are those of a good person.

Learn to love the principles and actions that make you a good person. And come back to these every time you stray.

Psychological Reflection

Don't feel bad if you ever stray from the right path, as long as you get back on it. It is necessary that you learn the importance of living according to your principles.

Have you ever made a mistake that enabled you to become a better person—perhaps more humble, understanding and compassionate?

How can you find yourself if you don't feel lost?

49

NOTHING LASTS FOREVER

Question/comment from a seeker:

I'm going through a difficult time. I don't know how long it will last and I need a message to cheer me up a bit.

Response from Marcus Aurelius (V–XXIII):

Remember that everything in this world is transient and can disappear very quickly.

Everything is constantly changing in an infinite number of ways, like a river that does not stop flowing—even the things that worry us or that we dislike.

Be patient and you will see that the things you disapprove of disappear and change, in the same way that everything else does.

Psychological Reflection

If nothing lasts forever, what is the point of worrying so much? Think about your past concerns, how they were resolved and how you feel about them now. Was it worth worrying so much?

How important will the things you worry about today be in five years? In ten years? If they won't be very important, isn't it better that you dedicate yourself today to what will remain relevant as time goes by?

50

THE EXCHANGE OF FAVOURS

Question/comment from a seeker:

It is very sad that when you do something for others, often people are quick to forget—they do not remember you or try to return the favour in the future. Why help people when they're so selfish?

Response from Marcus Aurelius (V–VI):

When you do someone a kindness, don't be on the lookout for an opportunity to have that courtesy reciprocated or think that that person owes you something.

It is better to act like the vine that expects nothing in exchange for producing grapes, the horse for running, the dog for finding prey or the bee for making honey.

Being a good person is part of your human nature, so don't look for an exchange of favours.

Psychological Reflection

We are used to the fact that nothing is free in this life, that one favour must be paid back with another. We have forgotten the pleasure that comes from doing something for another human being without demanding anything in return, simply acting out of the goodness of our heart and a desire to help.

When was the last time you did something for someone else without expecting anything in return and without thinking that you did that person a favour?

What are the gifts that you give to others? Who can you start helping with your actions today, if you decide to do so?

51

COMPASSION

Question/comment from a seeker:

There are people who have hurt me and do not deserve to be forgiven.

Response from Marcus Aurelius (VII–XXII):

As a human being, you can forgive and feel affection even for those who hurt you. Remember that we are all human, and those who act badly do so because their ignorance prevents them from making good decisions.

Life is short and, before long, we will all have disappeared from this world. Also, reflect upon the following: no one has actually done you any harm, because no one can undermine your principles or values, since these are two things that are completely within your control.

Psychological Reflection

If a child hurts us, we will probably not take it to heart because the child acts from a lack of understanding. We can think in the same way about our relatives and loved ones, even if it is more difficult to do so. But what if we had the same attitude towards everyone in the world?

What happens inside us when we accept the hurtfulness of others, learn not to be their victims and choose to pardon their ignorance?

Compassion does not mean being blind, it means loving despite being aware of the harm around us. A man once lost his inheritance when his mother and sister conspired against him. Though the betrayal made him bitter at first, he later sought legal help and consulted his spiritual guru, finding relief in both. He decided that if his mother or sister ever asked for forgiveness, he would grant it with a peaceful heart. But if they didn't, he would happily move on with his life. Forgiveness is not about ignoring the wrongs done to you; it is about letting go of resentment and reclaiming your peace of mind.

52

ACHIEVING THE IMPOSSIBLE

Question/comment from a seeker:

I do not achieve anything that I seek to accomplish. I am unable to quit smoking, I don't get promotions at work, I cannot find a good partner ... Is this my destiny?

Response from Marcus Aurelius (VI–XIX):

Do not assume that something is impossible to achieve just because it requires a lot of effort. If something is possible for other people, it is also within your reach.

You're better off thinking, 'If another human has managed to do and understand this, I can too.'

Psychological Reflection

Have you ever done something that you originally considered impossible to achieve? When something is very difficult for you or you think it is impossible, do you look to other people who have accomplished it to inspire you as role models? Do you really try to understand how others have done it so that you can do it too?

To be a teacher, you must first be a good learner.

53

POSITIVE INFLUENCES

Question/comment from a seeker:

How can I improve my relationships with others?

Response from Marcus Aurelius (VI–XLVIII):

Think regularly about the positive qualities of those around you: the energy of one person, the kindness of another, the generosity of a third …

You will realise that nothing makes us as happy and content as appreciating the virtues of those around us.

Psychological Reflection

As human beings, we are influenced by others. What impresses us influences how we see the world, and how we see the world influences how we feel. Our emotions influence what we do and the results we get.

Why, then, not allow ourselves to be influenced by the good qualities in the people around us?

What kind of people do you expose yourself to regularly? Are they a good influence on you? Observe what is going on in your head and your gut when you are engaging with these people, and you will find the answer.

54

FORTUNE AND MISFORTUNE

Question/comment from a seeker:

Why does this happen to me? Why now?

Response from Marcus Aurelius (XII–XIII):

It is strange and sometimes amusing to see how surprised people can be by life's events.

Psychological Reflection

We are not surprised to see the fortunes and misfortunes of others, but it amazes us when the same thing happens to us.

Almost everything that happens to others can also happen to you. Or do you think you are special and that nothing unpleasant can ever befall you, even if it afflicts everyone else in this process of learning called life?

55

DON'T LET OTHERS DECIDE FOR YOU

Question/comment from a seeker:

I find myself in a situation that causes me a lot of stress and I do not know whether to continue fighting and enduring it, or to seek change. Some people advise me to do one thing, others suggest something else, and in the end, I don't know how and what to decide …

Response from Marcus Aurelius (V–XXIX):

Sometimes, if there is a serious fire, it is necessary to escape. Why would you worry about acting to get out of that situation? As long as you are alive, you will remain free and no one can prevent you from doing what you consider right.

Psychological Reflection

If life forces you to leave or change something, so be it. But if there is no reason for change, do not let the others decide for you. It is you who is in the situation, so why should anyone else take the reins?

You are the CEO of your own life.

56

YOUR HAPPINESS DEPENDS ON YOU

Question/comment from a seeker:

How can I have good luck?

Response from Marcus Aurelius (V–XXXVI):

To be lucky is to have good habits of the soul, good impulses and good actions. In other words: think well, speak well and practise good deeds. All of this is within your control and will improve your good luck.

Psychological Reflection

Your happiness depends on you, your positive mindset and your choices. Only you can ensure that things go well for you in your own life. Good luck is luck that is within your control. What will you choose in order to feel luckier right here and now?

57

WHO CONTROLS YOUR MOOD?

Question/comment from a seeker:

Which is better? Being authentic and perceived as aggressive by others because you maintain your strong values, or trying hard to please others at the risk of becoming submissive?

Response from Marcus Aurelius (XI–XVIII):

You should avoid getting angry with others, and also refrain from meaninglessly praising them. Both attitudes are bad for co-existence in society and both can hurt you. Try to be authentic and true to yourself and don't let others disturb your peace of mind.

Psychological Reflection

Obsessing about others creates emotional dependence: if you let them hurt you, you will become sad or angry; if you let them admire you, your ego and your pride will grow. If you allow this to happen, your state of mind will be on an endless roller coaster, always responding to and depending on others.

Is there someone in your life who frequently controls your mood? How can you bring more balance to the situation so that it does not rob you of your inner peace?

58

DRINKING SALT WATER

Question/comment from a seeker:

What is your perspective on people who think that the purpose of life is only to enjoy it?

Response from Marcus Aurelius (VI–XXXIV):

Balance is necessary, because merely enjoying unlimited pleasure is what characterises thieves, immoral people and tyrants.

Psychological Reflection

Letting yourself be carried away by pleasure is like drinking salt water: the more you drink, the thirstier you become. Your mind and body will never be satisfied, and so it is better to aim for a healthy balance.

Is there any pleasure in your life that enslaves you? What can you do to improve the situation?

59

WHAT IS YOUR PURPOSE?

Question/comment from a seeker:

In the little free time I have, I try to have fun and relax. I don't have time to think about the meaning of life or other deep questions.

Response from Marcus Aurelius (VIII–XIX):

Everything in this world has a purpose. Do you think that human beings are born only to work and have fun?

Psychological Reflection

Often, we live from day to day, trapped in our daily routines, our obligations and our pleasures. And so we live week after week, year after year. We rarely stop to think about the meaning of our lives or why we are here.

What is the purpose of your life? It may be a difficult question to answer, but isn't it worth at least thinking about?

60

ACCEPT WHAT COMES

Question/comment from a seeker:

Life is very hard. One day you have everything, the next you lose it all. How can I live amid the uncertainty and instability in this world?

Response from Marcus Aurelius (X–XIV):

If you develop humility and educate your mind as a good philosopher does, you can tell destiny, 'Give me what you want and take away what you like.' You will not say this as a challenge; rather, your maturity will enable you to cooperate with the inevitable and strengthen your faith in life.

Psychological Reflection

If we ask something of life and it grants it to us, we are happy. If life doesn't provide it, we become sad. If our happiness depends on life fulfilling our wishes, is it happiness that can be depended on? Wouldn't we be better off not asking for anything and accepting what comes and goes with gratitude?

61

TO WHAT DO YOU ATTACH YOURSELF?

Question/comment from a seeker:

I suffer from anxiety because I am very materialistic. How can I develop a greater degree of detachment?

Response from Marcus Aurelius (VII–XXVII):

Pretend that what you don't have doesn't exist. It is better to value what you have: look at all the things you already possess and think about how much you would want them if you didn't have them. Try not to enjoy your possessions too much, to avoid overvaluing them and feeling upset if you ever lose them.

Psychological Reflection

Our mind works through attachment. According to the cognitive psychologist Walter Riso, 'Attachment is a mental and emotional (generally obsessive) connection to objects, people, activities, ideas or feelings, originated in the irrational belief that this connection will provide, in a unique and permanent way, pleasure, security or self-realisation.'

The more you get attached to something, the more difficult it will be to detach yourself from it. Analyse your attachments: to whom or what in your life are you too 'hooked'? Is there something that you can connect to that is not perishable?

62

GRABBING A HOT COAL

Question/comment from a seeker:

Sometimes, it is necessary to get angry. If you don't get angry, others won't take you seriously.

Response from Marcus Aurelius (XI–XVIII):

When you feel like you are starting to get carried away by anger, remember that it is not worth it. It is patience and kindness that define the human being. A person with these characteristics has real strength, guts and drive. Someone who is outraged and shows their displeasure does not have true strength.

Psychological Reflection

As the Buddha said, holding on to anger is like grabbing a hot coal with the intention of throwing it at another person; in the end it will be you who gets burnt.

Have you ever achieved something in your life by acting with anger or impatience? And if the answer is 'yes', was it worth doing this?

Marcus Aurelius encourages us not to get carried away by negative emotions. The price we pay for feeling this way and the price others have to pay for putting up with us are too high.

63

THE IMPORTANCE OF THINGS

Question/comment from a seeker:

How can I better manage my time? What activities should I spend less time on and vice versa?

Response from Marcus Aurelius (IV–XXXII):

The first step you need to take is to decide what is most important to you. When you know what your priorities are, you will give each activity the attention it deserves and, at the end of the day, you won't regret having paid too much attention to unimportant things.

Psychological Reflection

Do not give more importance to things, people and events than they really deserve. On the other hand, is there something in your life that deserves more time and dedication from you, which you are currently neglecting because you are obsessing about unimportant things?

64

FEELING GOOD HERE AND NOW

Question/comment from a seeker:

What do you recommend to disconnect from stress and relax? Should I go to the mountains, take a walk or do a retreat?

Response from Marcus Aurelius (IV–III):

Many people seek to relax in the countryside, on the coast or in the mountains. But going away doesn't make much sense, because if you wish to, you can withdraw into yourself whenever you want. You will not find as much serenity anywhere as you will find in your own soul.

Psychological Reflection

If you are not happy with yourself, you can be in any paradise on earth and still not be pleased. But if you're happy, it will not matter where you are.

65

PRACTISE DIFFICULT THINGS

Question/comment from a seeker:

Sometimes, I think that with the current circumstances, it is impossible to move forward and I should just 'throw in the towel'.

Response from Marcus Aurelius (XII–VI):

If a task seems impossible, spend more time practising it. Even the weaker hand, which struggles with many tasks, is able to perform them after training.

Psychological Reflection

What did you consider impossible to do until, after continuous practise, you did it? Think of a child and all the stages of learning they go through. The child does not think, 'It is impossible to walk.' Instead, they try as many times as necessary until they finally can.

66

ACCEPT WITH OPEN ARMS

Question/comment from a seeker:

What should I think or do when I am trying to control what I am not able to control?

Response from Marcus Aurelius (X–XXXV):

If one eye is healthy, it sees everything that can possibly be seen and does not say, 'I would like to see only green things.' That would be typical of a diseased eye.

In the same way, a healthy mind is ready for anything. If your mind expects that you will only experience good things, it would be like the diseased eye that only wants to see green.

Psychological Reflection

If an eye could have tastes and preferences, it would inevitably suffer every time it saw something that was not to its liking. Our mind has this ability to discern and judge, and it suffers as a result.

How would your well-being change if you always had a positive attitude and accepted everything that happened in your life with open arms?

67

OBSERVE YOURSELF FIRST

Question/comment from a seeker:

Should I help others work on their flaws?

Response from Marcus Aurelius (VII–LXXI):

The mature person focuses on their own self-improvement rather than those of other people.

It is possible to recognise your own weaknesses and improve them, because these are within your control. But it is absurd to expect the weaknesses and defects of others to disappear, as you cannot control these.

Psychological Reflection

Often, we see the faults of others more clearly than our own. Marcus Aurelius asks us to look at ourselves in the mirror, recognise our own 'evilness' (everything evil that comes from us and that we can avoid) and try to improve. We must focus our efforts on being better people, instead of judging others and trying to make them change.

You cannot separate yourself from external forces, but you can improve what comes from within—what is generated by your own mind. Instead of fighting against the 'evil' that you see in others, how about you work hard to become a good example for them?

68

DO THE BEST YOU CAN

Question/comment from a seeker:

I'm in a situation where the only thing I can do is to just let myself go and try to move on, no matter what. How could I reflect on my situation in order to feel less helpless?

Response from Marcus Aurelius (VII–LIII):

If God and fate put you in circumstances that you cannot change, but you act in the best possible way with what you have and where you are in that point in time, then you need not be afraid of anything.

Psychological Reflection

Always do the best you can. Contemplate the options and information that you have at any given moment, and make the decision that seems the best to you and that aligns with your values.

It is better to leave the consequences of your actions or decisions in the hands of 'the gods'. Why worry about the result, if you cannot control it?

69

IT'S NOT AS BAD AS IT SEEMS

Question/comment from a seeker:

I am afraid of the future.

Response from Marcus Aurelius (VIII–XXXVI):

Remember that the past and the future have no power over you.

Instead of thinking about the negative things that could happen to you, focus on your current situation and ask yourself: at this very moment, here and now, do I have a problem that is so serious that I cannot manage it? You will see that the present is always more manageable.

Psychological Reflection

Often, we suffer because of what happened in the past, or for what we think will come in the future but never does. If we focus only on the present moment, we may realise that there is nothing so serious that it cannot be managed.

Try to think of a past event that seemed more serious than it ultimately was. How do you feel now, thinking about it? What is happening in your life right here and now that may not be as serious as it seems?

70

ACCEPT HELP

Question/comment from a seeker:

Why am I so ashamed to ask for help?

Response from Marcus Aurelius (VII–VII):

Don't be ashamed to ask for help. Imagine that you are a soldier with a mission to accomplish. Would you abandon your mission if you are injured and limping and cannot fulfil it? Or would you ask a teammate for help, if that enables you to execute your task?

In many situations, asking for help can be the most logical and smart thing to do. There is no reason to feel embarrassed about making a wise choice.

Psychological Reflection

Sometimes, we have to accept our limits and know when to ask for help. That is not a weakness, but rather a strength.

How many things in your life have you been able to achieve only thanks to other people? Is there something in your life right now for which you could use the help of another person?

71

DO NOT OVERANALYSE

Question/comment from a seeker:

I don't understand why I have such bad luck in life. Why do all these negative things happen to me?

Response from Marcus Aurelius (VIII–L):

If the cucumber is bitter, throw it out. If there are thorns in your way, steer clear of them. Try to be practical. If there is something you can avoid, avoid it. For things you cannot change, accept them and do not ask, 'Why do these things happen?'

Psychological Reflection

Don't overanalyse things, as this will get you nowhere. Do the best you can and focus on what is up to you. If you get angry, offended or outraged by everything you think is unfair or bad in life ... will this change anything about the situation?

72

KNOW WHAT TO ASK FOR

Question/comment from a seeker:

What should I ask God for?

Response from Marcus Aurelius (IX–XL):

Either God has no power or He is almighty. If He has no power, why ask Him for anything? But if He has power, instead of asking him for something to happen or not happen, why don't you request that he grant you the ability to fear nothing, desire nothing and not feel upset about anything that occurs?

Psychological Reflection

If you don't believe in God, there is no point in asking Him for anything. But if you believe in Him, wouldn't it be better to ask Him to give you the strength and positive attitude you need to overcome anything that happens to you, rather than asking Him to simply make happen whatever you want?

73

YOU WILL NOT LIVE FOREVER

Question/comment from a seeker:

Should I live thinking about death or is it better not to reflect on that topic too much and simply enjoy life?

Response from Marcus Aurelius (IV–XVII):

Don't act like you have ten thousand years to live. Death weighs on you. While you are still alive, aim to be as good a person as you can be.

Psychological Reflection

Bronnie Ware, an Australian writer who worked for many years in palliative care, summed up the five most frequent regrets that people had on their deathbed.

People wished they had had the courage to do what they wanted to do, that they had worked less, that they had been brave enough to express their feelings, that they had kept better contact with their friends and that they had been happier.

We underestimate how long we have left to live and ignore death, thinking about it as something that happens to other people.

What would you change if you knew that you had little time to live? To whom or what are you not dedicating enough time, energy and love? What can you do about it?

74

WHY ARE YOU DOING IT?

Question/comment from a seeker:

I work hard and I am proud of it. I have been taught to pursue the goals I set for myself in life. I think that work gives you dignity.

Response from Marcus Aurelius (IX–XII):

Don't work just for the sake of working or for others to pat you on the back. You must have a strong sense of why you do the work you do.

Psychological Reflection

Do you work the right number of hours to do your duty or to do good for society? Or are you a person who dedicates their whole life to work, in order to please others, get a promotion or because you simply have no other purpose in life?

When you dedicate yourself to something, ask yourself what you are doing it for and if the value and importance of that task justifies the effort you put into it. Is there something in your life that deserves more or less dedicated time and energy?

75

THE MASTER OF DECEPTION

Question/comment from a seeker:

I have an important job and many people depend on me and my decisions. I can't think about the meaning of life and other similar questions, to which there are no answers anyway.

Response from Marcus Aurelius (VI–XIII):

Pride is a master of deception—when you think you're solving the most important issue in the world, that's exactly when it has you under its spell.

Psychological Reflection

Pride arises when we think we are more important than we are or when we place too much significance on something that is 'ours' such as our body, the opinions we have developed, the religion we have chosen, our home, our children or our profession. But all of this is a deception of our mind. As an Asian proverb says, you only possess what you cannot lose in a shipwreck.

What do you own that you could never lose in a shipwreck? What is really yours?

76

LOSS

Question/comment from a seeker:

Can we overcome the pain of losing a loved one? I find it impossible.

Response from Marcus Aurelius (IX–XXXV):

Loss is nothing but transformation.

Psychological Reflection

We are all afraid of losing something very valuable to us and, worse still, of losing someone. The fear of death is the mother of all fears. What can help you overcome that fear? Maybe faith?

You can only lose something if it belongs to you. And as mentioned in the previous reflection, you only own what you cannot lose in a shipwreck. If you think about it, there are very few things in life that you can actually lose because almost nothing is really yours.

Is there something in your life that you feel you have lost, but if you think about it, never actually belonged to you?

77

PASSIVITY

Question/comment from a seeker:

Better to do nothing than to do something and make a mistake.

Response from Marcus Aurelius (IX–V):

Doing nothing is also doing something. Do not delay an important decision or avoid acting because you think that things will resolve themselves. Often, those who do not act commit as much injustice as those who do take action.

Psychological Reflection

Sometimes, we may think that if we do nothing, we cannot make any mistakes. But what happens if you see a child drowning and you do not act? ... Or if you make a mistake and do not correct it or recognise your fault? ... Or if you do not think about the consequence of your actions and cause harm to others? ... We could think of many more examples.

Have you ever done wrong by failing to do, act or think about something?

78

ATTACHMENT

Question/comment from a seeker:

How can I avoid becoming attached to things or people?

Response from Marcus Aurelius (VIII–XXXIII):

Accept with humility and let go with ease.

Psychological Reflection

Luck, chance and destiny are completely out of your control. If your happiness depends on something that is not in your hands, it will always be a slave to uncertainty. Marcus Aurelius tells us that it is better not to get attached to anything that fortune gives us, and that we should not feel upset when luck seems to work against us.

If your happiness does not depend on what happens to you in life—what you gain or what you lose—but rather on an unshakable faith that everything has its purpose and it is all in the hands of a divine will, how could you be anything other than happy?

79

HOW TO LIVE A GOOD LIFE

Question/comment from a seeker:

If you had one last piece of advice to give me, what would it be?

Response from Marcus Aurelius (III–V):

Do not act against your will or without reflecting. Do not do anything that harms others or let yourself be carried away by your emotions and thoughts. Do not be proud of your words. Speak sparingly and don't do too many things at once.

Psychological Reflection

What can you do to live in a way that is more aligned with this last piece of advice from Marcus Aurelius?

BIBLIOGRAPHY

Aurelio, M. (1985). *Meditaciones*. Madrid: Alianza Editorial S.A.

VV.AA. (1888). *Obras de los moralistas griegos: Marco Aurelio - Teofrasto - Epicteto - Cebes*. Madrid: Librería de la Viuda de Hernando y Ca.

Castaneda, C. (2016). *The Teachings of Don Juan: A Yaqui Way of Knowledge*. Berkeley, CA: University of Califonia Press.

Dolan, S. L. (2011). *Coaching by values: A guide to success in the life of business and the business of life*. Bloomington, IN: IUniverse.

Riso, W. (2015). *How to Overcome Emotional Dependency*. Phronesis SAS.

Schindler, Dr. J. A. (2003). *How To Live 365 Days A Year*. Philadelphia: Running Press.

Ware, B. (2019). *Top Five Regrets of the Dying: A Life Transformed by the Dearly Departing*. Carlsbad, CA: Hay House.

Zavala, J. M. (2010). *Padre Pío: Los milagros desconocidos del santo de los estigmas*. Madrid: LibrosLibres.